HELSINKI DRIFT

ALSO BY DOUGLAS BURNET SMITH

Thaw (1977)
The Light of our Bones (1980)
Scarecrow (1980)
Living in the Cave of the Mouth (1986)
Ladder to the Moon (1987)
The Knife-Thrower's Partner (1989)
Voices from a Farther Room (1993)
Two Minutes for Holding (1995)
The Killed (2000)
Chainletter (2001)

HELSINKI DRIFT

travel poems

DOUGLAS BURNET SMITH

Douglas Burnet Smith

Porcepic Books
an imprint of

Beach Holme Publishing
Vancouver

*Victoria
28/04/'02*

First Edition

This book is published by Beach Holme Publishing, 226–2040 West 12th Avenue, Vancouver, B.C. V6J 2G2. *www.beachholme.bc.ca* This is a Porcepic Book.

The publisher gratefully acknowledges the financial support of the Canada Council for the Arts and of the British Columbia Arts Council. The publisher also acknowledges the financial assistance received from the Government of Canada through the Book Publishing Industry Development Program (BPIDP) for its publishing activities.

The Canada Council | Le Conseil des Arts
for the Arts | du Canada

BRITISH
COLUMBIA
ARTS COUNCIL
Supported by the Province of British Columbia

Editor: Michael Carroll
Design and Production: Jen Hamilton
Cover Art: Detail of *Keitele* by Akseli Gallen-Kallela. Oil on Wood. © National Gallery, London, England. Used with permission.
Author Photograph: Bernice MacDonald

Printed and bound in Canada by AGMV Marquis Imprimeur

National Library of Canada Cataloguing in Publication Data

Smith, Douglas, 1949-
  Helsinki drift

Poems.
"A Porcepic book."
ISBN 0-88878-429-5

  I. Title.
PS8587.M526H44 2002   C811'.54   C2002-910163-8
PR9199.3.S55153H44 2002

For Alison →
all good Things,
all ways,

CONTENTS

Douglas

Ready to be anything in the ecstasy of being ever.
—Sir Thomas Browne

I've been things and seen places.
—Mae West

I
TIED BOAT

LATE DEPARTURE

(i) *Eleventh-Century Japanese Body Armour, Heathrow Airport*

Jets taxi
the tarmac
like slugs.

In a smeared display
case, dragons
swirl on a jade breastplate,
spew clouds over Fujiyama—
black, thick, etched
smoke swallowing
plum trees, surprised
farmers.

Jaded passengers
scurry, purchase
flight insurance,

carry-on bags filled
with the end
of the twentieth century.

(ii) *Bodhidarma Crossing the Blue River on a Reed*
(Chinese, Eighth Century, Artist Unknown)

each act
a cloud inconceivable
not to be
emptied
out of so
float
on the fiction
of the current

ARRIVAL LOUNGE ANXIETY ANTI-HAIKU

destinations
ricochet
over the red
shoulder bag
no one claims

LAKE DISTRICT RHYME, STONE COTTAGE

Mountain grosbeaks scorch early apple boughs;
Culvert echoes drown a rumbling train;
Snow asks forgiveness all the way to clouds—
And the kettle on the stove has the nerve to complain!

CLOUDS OVER TEIGNMOUTH
(KEATS'S APPARITION ANTI-HAIKU)

tubercular,
  they crave
the blood-drawn sunset
  that pales
like a crazed face

TENNYSON DOWN

Black medick, sea beet, spear thistle,
pellitory of the wall—the wind
comes up from the Channel wild over cliffs
and pushes these flowers
flat.

Lean
into the wind. Step over
mole barrows, tawny mole pebbles.
Hope for the ghost of the poet
to waddle into view
like some swan
in a black cape,
walking stick,
prim nurse beside him
bustling in furbelows.

But there's just a cross, a cold, useless
iron fence around it, far off
a black freighter going grey.

Isle of Wight

LOCH FYNE

At the edge of it,
you find the one small stone
that has been there since
smoothness won—
a bracelet's pink barn,
a polished steeple.

Walking into it,
ice-fiery currents peel
your knees.

Grace
deepens with every numbing step.

Kintyre

TIED BOAT

Who,
tired of surface, tied
that white boat, left it
to float by the spiderleg pier?

Only dark birds
know who let it rot
over itself, mirror its
oarlessness and the one thin seam
that suddenly

like a mouth

opened to allow everything
oceanic in.

KEATS HOUSE, HAMPSTEAD

Bring me a candle, Brown, and let me see this blood.
                              —February 3, 1820

A little swoon
by a lilac

and a screen
of Victorian trees, laurel
and yew

is given over
to his low fence,
the hedge of laurustinus
and China roses,

mulberry shade.
A paltry nightingale,
coughing words,
a dark-spotted
handkerchief:

"sitting and sobbing"
at the end
of Well Walk.

Words like
baleful and *timbral*
seem to write themselves

on thick paper
he used for travel

notes, silhouettes,
coughing anguished
slang. Surgery

of the wind
squeaking
out his lung,

the one still
responding—

dark pendant,
eloquent membrane

exhaling candlelit
letters into the air.

II
A POSTAGE STAMP

AMSTERDAM SHORT LIST

Sky the romantic amber of postcards.

Glassed-in
tour boats churn the canals,
scouring sepia hotels
with glaring spotlights.

Then a houseboat for cats.
The captain, in my jet-lag dream,
confessed
to having had sex with a variety
of farm animals.

And that he'd enjoyed it.
They "did not talk back,"
just shit on the knees of his pants
and his hands.

Black-and-white chaos of a pigeon-feeding station.
Someone, near dark, near the back
of the tour boat, muttering, "Get the gun, Elmo."

In several languages
the guide recalled the exact measure
of tanks and humiliation.

Sky a stupified ochre.

263 PRINSEGRACHT

Dazed in the Rijksmuseum, drawn
deep into still lives.
Vermeer's *The Cook*,
the woman in placid blue
pouring milk into a bowl,
a window's graded light
falling on the white plate
near her hands—
her simple act
miraculous. Paint

has become warmth I crave at dusk
in the rainy canals and shivery alleys of young junkies.
Reflected by lamplight—streetcars floating past,
houseboats and bicycles distorted on wavy mirrors—
everything's a bluish-yellow, a powder
ground between two stones, a moon egg
cracked into it to make a paste
called Amsterdam, glazed at sunrise
because the dark has left in a flushed urgency.

I send you this postcard of the false
bookcase, third floor, 263 Prinsegracht, now
a museum, behind which, for eighteen months,
Anne Frank was hidden.
When I walked through it, schoolkids were clustered around
photographs of the camps, pointing and giggling.
Faces in cattle cars, grim buildings.

I wondered what colour
Anne's eyes had been,
what hand she had written with.
I imagined her mother
pouring milk into a bowl
while some duteous banker granted a loan
to a man who had informed "the authorities"
about someone buying enough at the market
for two families.

It's grown almost too dark to write.

In a few minutes I board the train to Ghent
where I'll see van Eyck's huge altar:
The Righteous Judges and Knights of Christ.

A POSTAGE STAMP

Everyone knows the streets of Venice
aren't streets so much as alleys,
some two feet wide, and about as long,
and even those have names,
Corte Sconta, Detta Arcana,
every name stencilled in black against white
rectangles on olive walls, an arrow
pointing to a church,
a fountain.

More than anything, I remember
those signs—more than the canals chopping
at the rose facades that arch San Marco
out of their shadows like seductive eyebrows
over sloe lids. More than
those twin gold robots hammering stiff time
in the bell tower, mangy pigeons flowing
over the piazza, a feathered oil spill.

After compulsory sights—the Doge's tacky
palace, the Bridge of Sighs—get lost.
Ignore signs. Just walk
until you're hungry. Fried squid
and a jug of cheap wine in a two-table outdoor café
under a washline of bleached sheets—
these can help you stop dying for a while.
The owner's one-eared cat will come and sit on your lap
as you sip espresso and listen
to a disc jockey's voice
fade out

of a window somewhere.
You hear the latches of shutters
one by one close out afternoon heat, you watch
a few blackbirds flit
from one obsolete TV aerial to another.
All this is as exquisite
as Titian's *Presentation of the Virgin*.

You print addresses neatly
on postcards, mimicking those letters
on the sign for the nearest piazza.
You send a small moment
away, convinced a thing as light
as a postage stamp
can carry the weight of Venetian stone
across water.

ON A BRIDGE OVER THE ADIGE

For maybe an hour
I had the muddy slowness of the Adige
to myself. Then suddenly
a swarm of preschoolers, shrieking
in primary colours. Climbing everywhere.
A few quiet ones examined
rusted iron rings (for boats)
in the old stones.

Their teacher smiled apologetically
and brushed them across the bridge
inside the church of San Antonio.

The thin pigment of the Italian morning
is beginning to dry.
I have to write this down quickly
before it hardens into memory.

Verona

SCALLA DELLA RAGIONE

Piazza Brà, dusk, sidewalk tables. Sparrows
gather at my feet for crumbs. Contemptuous,
waiters sweep small tips onto small plates
with the heels of their hands—
they think that I, with my pathetic
Italian, am another stupid American,
and they have every reason to think so, except
I have less use for the Americans here than they have.

To my right, the arena of Verona
is crumbling, quietly, as it has every evening
for the past two thousand years.
Terra-cotta roofs
glow dull red
with the little of the sun left in them.
The sparrows return to nests
in cracks under leafy eaves.

Dante stares at everyone lingering in cafés
from across the piazza, but no one bothers to notice
a great poet undignified by pigeons.
And no one bothers to notice cypresses
catching fire
in front of the fountains
as the lights of the city come on.

Under this bridge, wind
makes its final declaration.
Buildings in the distance have begun to hover.

(Just as I finished that sentence, a wasp
hovered over my pen hand.)

Now the last of the light
is climbing down the Stairway of Reason
near the tiny church of Sant'Anastasia,
having learned patience at the top,
and not much else.

FIESOLE LAMENT

Profiteroles and chocolate-dusted cappuccino won't lift
just anyone beyond the terrace
of the Ristorante Aurora, or the clock tower
striking time from another century,
and that goes double
for those slow lovers walking under forty-foot cedars
beside the San Francesco Monastery, white white
columns and white white hands, her dress dragging violet
down blue marble steps laid 1216, and then, defiant,
two butterflies rise also white out of hill grass, flight paths
intersecting in her hair above dark eyes, small caves
from a Dalí lithograph of *La Dolce Vita*,
as the lovers take one last sunset look
over the hills of Tuscany, unaware
there's no chance that what they have won't die. Like hell
it won't it won't it won't stars insist coming on
to each other
above the lonely coliseum.

TUSCAN SCORPION

Her leg was dead.

She'd had to drag herself
across the blistering, cracked terrazzo stones
back to the villa
through what she'd half hallucinated
in the rising heat—
sunflower field, poppy field (eyelid-
red), one for each of his
hands, later hoisting her
down from the sweat-soaked bed
to a cool tile floor, and heaven.

She'd remember the day only
as a strange, momentary
ice-burning sole
as she stepped toward the trellis,
roses, "to bend a branch,
to smell petals," now
fallen. She couldn't sleep and he'd
gotten up to throw a shoe
at a manic crow
on the stone wall.
She'd followed, thought she was following
his laughter:
if she'd just walked the other way...

Soon delirium
detached itself from the sound
of her throat uncoiling

in his neck.
What he feared
crusted to the corners of her eyes,
small bubbles
at one corner of her mouth.

Paralyzed. She couldn't
tolerate not feeling
her own terror,
tried to locate it
in her "heel,"
that throbbing, rose, watery pulp
down there, out of reach,
floating around
a white blister
puckered at the edge of their story,
now the centre,
as though the story had needed
something, to be stung
in the extremities.

if she had just…

Their holiday clotted
around antibiotics
and the veined hands
of an old woman in black
crossing herself and placing cool linen
on the forehead, over the eyes
that didn't open
for three days, and then merely

at the insistence
of jet engines, demonstrations
in mimed Italian about the seat belt
that secured her into blanketed dreams
she'd never remember,

in dense cloud,
holding a stranger's hand for hours or days,
unfaithful to venom.

III

IN ANOTHER STATION OF THE MÉTRO

The trip doesn't exist that can set you beyond the reach
of cravings, fits of temper, or fears.
—Seneca

FOREIGN HANDS

Of course, I get lost
my first few hours in Paris.
(I don't *really* get lost, at least
not on the métro, but when I have to climb
stairs back up to daylight,
leaving logical grids behind,
I get lost easily enough.)

Notre Dame—
the guidebook says walk *up* the hill, so I do.
But I'm on the wrong hill,
or mistake a slight rise
for the hill I can't see. At the same time,
I'm trying to find the Hôtel Esmérelda,
expecting some desk clerk's parody of Lon Chaney,
dripping eye, nifty hump,
but I find myself
in front of the cathedral, and it's throbbing
with tour buses.

Of course, I'm not ready for Notre Dame
(nobody ever is), those busy buttresses, gargoyles glowering
and drooling over the cobblestones, arched windows
sending sunlight down through their quilted prisms
in lozenges bright on the knee-worn floor.
I'm not ready, either, for that crowd blocking the bridge
off the *île*, watching those kids on skateboards
wheel up plywood ramps and fly
over a row of seven toppled trash cans.
I just want to wash the métro

off my face, stare out
a shuttered window at *la tour*
beyond the clutter of rooftops.
I don't need the marbled eyes
of a beggar
brought that close to my own
as I round the corner onto rue Saint-Jacques,
and I don't need to disbelieve his hands
are that soft
when he touches my wrist
as I bend to put some change
in his bowl.

When I stand in my room, finally,
looking down at my hands
in warm water, I'll know
their invisible foreignness was to him certainly not
the best-remembered accident of the day.

BAR LES PIPOS

In the ruined Latin Quarter, about five minutes' walk
from the Panthéon, rue de la Montagne
and Sainte-Geneviève. A small *tabac*
with dark wooden tables and chairs,
hand-carved oak bar,
long benches with red leather backs lining three walls, another
wall of windows facing the street.
You know the type—a little accordion music,
roll credits,
and you're in a 1930s Renoir film,
extras sleeping it off
in cardboard boxes in the alley.

It's around noon.
Two men stand at one end of the bar
talking to the owner, another
stands alone, smoking a thin cigar,
looking anxiously out the windows,
as if he's expecting a raid.
The owner disappears into the back, reappears
holding a green bottle in one hand.
He says something to the two men
and they laugh a great laugh.
They look at me and wink. I smile,
missing the joke entirely.
A young man and woman walk in, sit down
at a table, and order sambuca, then begin
to neck ferociously. An old woman,
who must be a regular, hunches in and asks for *la clé*,
trundles upstairs, trundles back down some minutes later,

nods her white head scarf goodbye. The couple
continue necking, she undoes the top few buttons
of his shirt, enough so she can kiss
a nipple. They order more sambuca
and start arguing about cinema.
Hitchcock and Truffaut. Coppola.
They go back to necking. Now his hand is disappearing
down the back of her jeans. She looks like
a young Baudelaire, stern eyes, a little manic.

A century or so earlier, contemplating suicide,
Baudelaire actually could have walked in here,
all in black, a copy of Poe under his arm,
ordered an absinthe
to kill the jitters from a three-day hash binge,
and written a poem
about the angels with feral grins,
long tongues, and claws,
driving merciful spikes
through the throats of the extras
fitfully asleep outside.

MONA LISA HANGING IN THE LOUVRE ANTI-HAIKU

it is so guarded
a smile,
deadened,
even behind bulletproof
glass

IN ANOTHER STATION OF THE MÉTRO

If you take Paris for granted, you can become
a pointillist dot in the rain
on top of Eiffel's dowsing girders.
You can decide not to visit
Picasso's first studio,
and sit in front of it on the curb,
watching the evening wash down its rose-grey walls
with a blue brush.

At midnight you can watch four people calmly crawl
out of the windows
of a flipped-over Citroën
that's just sparked its way across the wet boulevard,
about a hundred metres
on its roof,
in front of les Invalides.
A pretender,
you can sit late on rue des Écoles,
nursing café au lait, and hear Notre Dame
come out of itself, eleven times, twelve,
and later, just once, barely,
after turning out the light in a room
of cracked plaster and cockeyed shutters.

But next morning, when you descend into the métro—
at Saint-Michel, thinking of faces and wet petals,
Paris will have grown a little haggard,
each bell-shaped hour just beyond sleep
having sifted down like soot over the Seine
because a legless woman

will be lying on the tiles
of the tunnel to the train.
To say that she is "dressed" in rags
would be a true crime. To say her rags
look like torn crepe paper, and are about as warm,
would be dispassionately descriptive enough
that Christ might come back
and go after you with a gun.

If you have the small courage to stop
in the midst of all the well-heeled echoes
and faces, and drop
a coin in her cardboard box,
you may have to suffer missing a train
on your way to see Léger at the Pompidou.
But later on, when Paris is lighting up again,
you can scrub the soot off your face
and rub your two swollen feet
with both good hands.

DRAGON TATTOO AND PIERCING

Rue de la Verrerie

Six steps down from the street,
through an old black-latched oak door,
into the dank stone
of 16th-century Paris,
21st-century rock pulsing
out of hidden speakers,
black-light posters, incense, Moroccan
bead necklaces, ankle bracelets, tattoo samples,
photos of ears, tongues, noses, penises, labia—piercings
priced by the body part.

Three thousand wasps
sting my earlobe
all at once. "Your *horreur*
is over now, *monsieur*," he says,
the young man with the ring
through his lip
who's just jabbed
a needle through my skin.

But it's not.
A red fishing line
of blood arcs
above my neck
and spluts against brick.

He's gone to answer the phone.
Blood pours down my throat.
My T-shirt's a reluctant blotter.

Blood splotches onto the onion-paper-covered bench
I'm seated on, then seeps
into my jeans.

"*Merde!*" This gets the guy's attention,
since the more polite
"*Monsieur, s'il vous plaît*" didn't.

He wraps a towel around my head,
mops my neck with a washcloth, removes
the towel, removes
my T-shirt, rewraps the towel,
wrings my T-shirt out
in a sink of cold water,
hangs it over a chair to dry,
looks at this turbaned coward, and says, reassuringly,
confirming my midlife vanity,
"*C'est normale.*"
"Yeah, right."
Beside us, a woman who's just had her left nipple
and her navel pierced and connected with a small chain
is showing them to friends who have arrived
but who are looking more at the towel on my head
than at the red swellings
of her nipple and navel.
"*Vous les aimez?*" she asks them.
They nod, glancing in my direction,
then disappear upstairs, trying not to smile.

The needle guy whispers in the woman's ear,
gesturing in my direction.
She nods.

She walks over to me.
"I am helping your pain," she says,
putting her hands on my shoulders,
easing me onto my back
like a baby. Her nipple's
redder now. Her navel's plum blue.
"Close please your eyes." She unwraps
the towel, places one palm
on my forehead, one palm
in the hollow of my chest.

"Now we are breathing."
I match her long, slow breaths
and my sternum is still warm,
my forehead cool
when I open my eyes.

How long has she been gone?

My pain
is a tiny pulse.

"Deux cents francs, monsieur,"
says needle guy.
"We take all your cards."

AKHMATOVA'S PARIS RECURRING NIGHTMARE ANTI-HAIKU

rain, slashing hard
against the window.
Stalin's fists
smashing
through the glass

PLAYING SCRABBLE WITH TRISTAN TZARA AT THE TROIS MAILLETS

He agrees to play in English,
saying it doesn't matter
which language we play in—
"They are all the same, languages.
They are mud."
"Mud?"
"*Exactement!* Mud!" and he orders
couscous with Algerian wine.

I go first, choosing seven tiles
from the maroon box.
Incredible! Six of the seven,
with a quick reassembly,
spell *zephyr*—
triple-letter score for *z*,
magnificent opening,
double-word score—52!
Which Tzara demeans
by holding his nose and
spewing a mouthful of couscous
across the room.

A crowd gathers.

His turn. He snaps his suspenders
snat-tat,
picks up seven tiles,
shakes them in cupped palms,
closes his eyes,

places the letters one by one
on the board under the Z
like so   O
                               E
                               S
                               I
                               B
                               I
                               X

The crowd applauds.
"Zoesibix?" I ask. "That's a word?"
"Mais oui!"
"But what does it mean?"

"It means what it means!" His lip curls.
The crowd murmurs approval.

"Right," I say in my best poker voice
and place all my new letters
after the *X*:
P C T A M H E.
Tzara looks at me, eyebrows arched,
incredulous.
"The plural," I explain.

The crowd gasps a big gasp.

"Ah, bon!" he spits, producing
a revolver from the inside pocket of his coat,
holding it against his temple,
finger trembling on the trigger,
"You are obviously a grandmaster!"

TOO LATE FOR STARS

Moon like a skinned pear, halved and speckled
by birch leaves, sinking
over the chimney pots
of rue Burnouf, Belleville, 5:00 a.m.
Footsteps in the lightening dark
come toward the window,
a scuffled summons from
three floors down.
A whitish blotch, an Impressionist
face looks up the ravine
of buildings past mine, shopping
much too late for stars.

PLACE DE LA CONTRESCARPE (I)

It's enough
to sit and watch

the linden-shaded fountain's
eight arcs

never fill
the stone pool.

LES PHILOSOPHES

The bar, that is. Rue du Temple, the Marais, sunset.
A large beer, while everyone heads home after work.
It's my time to write. *"Dix francs, monsieur,"* a hand opens
on my notebook near my glass,
pushed away before I even understand,
the waiter in black vest, white shirt, black tie, scolds
the beggar woman off, past the gay clubs, past the boutiques,
the notices
for natural gas lines they'll lay
in the gentrification
of what used to be a perfect swamp.

PLACE DE LA SORBONNE

There's a Gypsy kid grovelling convincingly at my shoes,
mumbling on the hot asphalt
with his hand out,
red pants torn off at the knees,
no shoes, filthy feet.
At the mouth of *la place*, they're playing Vivaldi, well-dressed
university students—three cellos, six violins—horseshoed
between two motorcycles and a statue of Auguste Comte.

The notes float over the heads of everyone
seated on yellow chairs at white tables,
pour off the facade
of l'église de la Sorbonne,
spiral back to us, as the Gypsy kid
scores a coin or two, smiles,
goes into his crying act at the next table,
evening sunlight speckling walls
through the rust-edged leaves of parched trees.

JULY 14

It's hot. Hot enough
for black grime
on the floor of this métro car
to liquefy, turn to tar,
and coat the bare soles
of a woman kneeling
with a cardboard sign
j'ai faim, s'il vous plaît
pour mes enfants
two ragged four-year-olds
clinging to her skirt with one hand,
holding the other out, proffered, cupped, piercing
dark brown eyes trained
on money pouches and cameras
of the obvious tourists
in walking shoes,
on their way to dinner,
trying to ignore the mother's
invading sign, not noticing the quick hand
sidewinding along one man's belt
and inside his sport jacket
just before the car doors
close, the three of them
gone, *poof*, a magic act,
the doors sealing their audience
in, the man's hand now held
in a Napoleonic grimace
inside his jacket,
convinced his wallet must still be there,
not in some trash can

outside Concorde,
his money stuffed in the children's underwear
in case they're caught ducking under turnstiles
on their way back down to hot trains, sticky floors,
pitying and fearful faces.

PLACE DE LA CONTRESCARPE (II)

At the Irlandais, the next bar over,
the *cocktail du mois*
is Bulldog + Tequila = Le Freud.

Later, a dream of pigeons
descending over Trocadero
to attack the pope, their beaks
jabbing his eyes out
while *la jeunesse mondiale*
all 600,000
watch and pray.

PLACE DES ABBESSES

Clustered shade trees, pigeons, bells,
dog bark, thunder, neon-blue bar sign's
loose connection static;

Hendrix guitar chords, Heineken cans
rolling, Day-Glo martyrs, leather martyrs, everywhere
martyrs on mopeds;

Michelin guides, rain troughing
off the métro stairs' glass shelter
to *la Butte par la rue Lépic*, bells
muffled, sun break;

Docs and backpacks, ripe sunburns, mobile
phone-walking one-sided conversation:
*"La possibilité de l'amour, peut-être
en septembre en Corse"*;

litter scrape, bells, holy car alarm
hiccoughing, stale wind stuttering
in the shadow of Montmartre.

HAIKU DOUBLE

In heat
whose waves

would impress
the Bedouin

an olive-skinned woman
in lemon linen

slowly glides, *un vent frais*,
across the deserted square.

SONG OF SYNTAX AT LA CHOPE

Place de la Contrescarpe III

Why should I care
about just where

an adjective goes?
"Beautiful" can lie, I suppose,

anywhere,

either after or before,
fickle modifier

of the hair that flares
down her shoulders,

bare.

MEDICI FOUNTAIN, LUXEMBOURG GARDENS

Couples flank the long, fluid rectangle, shaded
dark, dark green by two stolid

plane trees and an ivy-arched
trellis. Pudgy carp, mottled

orange and white, mouth cliché capital O's.
A cautious wind carries away leaves

on just enough reluctant water spilling,
collecting, sliding, retreating, filling

a lower pool, where the gathered sound
conveniently dissolves in its own

slighted persistence and is never
ever quite sufficient to answer

for itself, nor for the lovers, silent, naked,
still, a tier above: Acis and Galatea, stretched

out flawless in white marble. He's
leaning on hip and elbow. She's

reclined against his muscled thigh
bent to support her whole body's sigh

of languorous satisfaction. And her eyes,
though closed, must know his tender gaze

will fall forever only on her face,
while ours includes Polyphemus,

jealous cyclops crouched in a rage
above them on the granite ledge

they trust has lent them perfect shelter
from a world whose petty gods conspire

against Love with hideous success. Of course,
they're dead wrong: he'll wreck their peace. Unless—

look again at their smooth, luminous skin;
yes, it's clear: desire's its own ageless protection.

ALÉSIA
à L.A.

Here I am in Paris being miserably lonely.
> —Kenneth Koch, "Currency"

I   BAGATELLE, BOIS DE BOULOGNE

Our Lady of Boulogne the Lesser
rises out of gold-tipped
reeds in *le jardin japonais*, drifts
as pond mist
in a histrionic Ophelian gown,
lily-strewn, toward the slate
mansard roof of *le restaurant du parc*,
the restored mansion where Napoleon and the Duc de Berry
studied the flight strategies
of imported butterflies.

An immodest rain
hunts the gravelled paths
for nostalgia
under chestnut trees and rose
trellises, toward l'Orangerie
and a peacock's cries. Sparrows
bivouac beside our table
on chair backs, flutter, and twitter
down for crumbs on the dampened French dirt.

The long-leftover grey
of the Merovingian air
concentrates the last hours

of June on your brow,
the small scar
perfectly arced there
like a pared
thumbnail, raised only
slightly, blond, blonder
than the Belgian beer with whisky
you turn and turn
in its glass, impatiently,
with one hand, twirling
a broken vine with the other.
For you, silence after the peacock
is the lost gasp of air
at your own birth, doctor
and mother collaborating to close
off your lane to the shallow, lighted
end of the canal, cutting
in and reaching in and pulling
you out, an errant
vessel, airless, objected to, carefully
objectified later in the typescript
of a hospital certificate.

White acorn globes
come on in the shadows
in threes. We've stopped reaching
across the gap of language, shrugging
and nodding our translated misunderstandings.

Rain pocks the dust around our sheltered feet.
The waiters move inside.
There's a pause in the bird traffic through the leaves.

You look up, beyond a copper
beech, to find sanctuary, a blue patch
in the clouds that matches
the size of the gaze
I'm abandoned by.

It's a clearing I can't see,
and you breathe your word
for it, and leave me
behind, excommunicant, trifling,
trying to cast everything in the future tense.

II   Pont des Arts

The Seine's a shimmering
scar. I could stand
above it here, staring, all night
at your face, wanting
more and more
and more the posturing dark
silence of the Louvre
on one side, and l'Académie Française
on the other, to keep all this
from being impossible.

And I want the tentative
agreement I've made with the river
to include your two hands
holding back
whatever wedge of light
is insinuating its way here,
unreasonable and unmerciful,

the arch their bones make
cradling my temples, the nave
of some small, protective, heretic
cathedral.

III   PLACE DE FÜRSTEMBERG

English words
over the phone
in that accent
I'm a sap for. Say

anything. It's a hymn
and I've got the call.
I'll meet you anywhere, even
on wobbly metaphorical
knees with no promise of paradise
regained, last night's
arm-in-arm emptied street, the white-globed
lampposts under the paulownias'
leaves still as aces
in the clinging humidity.

It could have been 1699. In his scarlet tunic
le cardinal could have been pacing,
sleepless, three ragged thieves manacled
in the pillory in rue de l'Abbaye
unrepentant, cursing him, predicting
his death, at the net, on the monastery tennis court.
Forty-love.

We stopped where Delacroix

died in 1863. These places
are nothing for you.
Streets are streets, not
miracles. My arm perhaps
just an arm. But your face

was a luminescent gift
and I knew your mouth
was going to taste like
what we'd drunk spilled back to the earth,
the moist night air, a bitter
secret in the dark.

IV   MÉTRO PLAISANCE

I'm trying to make my mouth make sounds
that will break my ears' English habits.

Pursing and puckering, my lips
fatigue, fail, fool no one

when I pretend I'm native.
And these onomatopoeic

expletives—*oeuff! pheuht!*—
they dangle in the air moments

after you release them, but I can't
round them up. They stay

strays. Mostly I opt
for pet silence, and fidget,

shy and ignorant, grovelling
in awe of bilabial fricatives.

What I want to get right
are the irregular verbs,

ones that can decode
this selfish ache for bliss,

preserve it, make of it a tasteful confiture:
impertinent, bold, tart.

V   IN THE MIDDLE OF THINGS

I pray the Tin Man
won't make a stiff entrance

in search of his hat
instead of his heart, having heard

there's one like it here,
overhead, the sieve you've rigged

splintering the light
from the bare bulb,

a mock chandelier
in your two-hundred-year-old

room. Regular
verbs become laser

pleas, tiny shattered
orders, shuddered

and perforated directions
for the paired

squadron of our hands
pressing the dark

fate of one palm relentlessly
into the dark fate of the other.

VI   Alésia

You've got a set of kids' afterglow stars
pasted on the ceiling, an indoor
galaxy over your bed. Turn
the light out—
black holes
and recognizable glitter.
Parce que
je ne peux pas voir les étoiles à Paris.

(But I see them
everywhere. Even the gutter's
a Milky Way of swirling
planet wrappers, rings of paper, bright
moon rinds, a glimmering
soup of space junk
floating down rue du Général Leclerc.)

They're gone by morning.

But you shine a little,
stepping out of the bath
as if it were a shell.

VII   RUE DES SUISSES

I'm deeply committing to memory
what I can't take home:

new love words, night
touches, surprise daybreak tastes.

Ambush of evening perfume. My name
pronounced the only way

it could ever have been meant
to be: vowels lengthened,

rounded to sheer dove sound.
And I'm coming, slowly, to accept

that grotesque glare on your face
as you work to make it conceal

the pleasure you're digging around for
where we're coiled and claimed.

VIII   VETO

At one end of a métro station
                 the sign
promising CORRESPONDANCES, at the other, nothing

You're somewhere
standing above the gleam of rails,
near the edge of a long cliff of people,
some probably on their way
to see impatient lovers, to explain
betrayals or have betrayals
explained to them.

Suddenly there's the expected shock
of wind making its way out of the tunnel,
almost biblical in its swift indifference,
pushing infernal air
just a few degrees cooler at the edges
out of the darkness

and into the sallow light of the station, glazing
garish Parisian billboards and wall tile
with a sickening fresco sealant, absorbed
into the air, damp and pallid,
as the horse eye of the train
blinks blindly open and blindly
shut, vaulting out of the dark,
shouldering into the light, passing
the first few ghostly faces
with a stammering roar, the wind
fanning those faces unconsolingly,
no matter how much grief
each face projects and reflects
in the sectioned glass
that hasn't reached you yet, poised

as you are three-quarters of the way down
the platform, still
a little too far off to feel
the full force of the wind.
But the vibration
          is coming up through your feet

like a proof for some tired
debate between philosophical abstraction
          and empirical reality, which is
merely exaggerating your useless existence,
          tedious desolation, opening it
up absurdly over you
like a tattered umbrella,

and you're staring down at the rails,
knowing you've got lots of time, *lots*
of time, before the wind finally
reaches you, staring as intently
as you are, and feeling a moment
stretch and almost tear as intensely as you are,
          that there may as well be thousands
of acres of track for the train to cover

          before it reaches even your
shadow, so you stare
at the tracks calmly
          and say to yourself

          take the step, and a synapse
starts to close in your right hip,
and the train is still

a comfortably elongated distance
away, far enough
for the hip to swivel in slow motion
in its socket, a knee
to flex and unlock, a foot to leave the platform,
        and the rest of you, thinking
and seeing and breathing in the purest light,
        the rest of you, the last
        of you, follows,
and then leads, tumbling
        into translucence,
the black translucence of wind and rails
        and train that crescents over you
with a plain, muffled, quotidian crescendo…

                    Years ago.

As I sit here in the early light,
bees disembowelling the daisies outside,
summer bird calls tapering off,
in a country you'd never thought about then
but are flying toward now
over an ocean already in a stronger light, where
"unspoiled natural beauty" and unextinguishable
provincialism chasten the Nova Scotia air
        and tighten like a reef knot
        around my neck, returned,
        not even a week from your bed and the rapture
        of the short paragraph
of declarative sentences we composed
        in two languages
        over thirty days,

one sentence a day, unrevised and
unfinished, a whole paired life's
to-be-continued melodrama uncontained
                            within it, the centre
your remembering, in disbelief and certainty,
standing on that platform about to take the step.

        In the August dawn, trying
to imagine you in another state, invisible,
            negligible, impossible, not
            there (and therefore
            none of this as well), trying
to delete your desire
for darkness, crossing out
verse after verse intent on a resolution,
            an explanation, finally
realizing there is none, was
            none, that there is only
endless revision, and that at some moment
in the absent click of that synapse
            on that overcrowded platform, something
in you understood this and managed to step back,
the wind whooshing over you
            in a blank rush, the train
stopping stupidly in front of you, doors
            rumbling open, and you
putting one foot waveringly
            down in a clean, enlightened dread,
            and then the other, doors
rumbling shut behind you and rattling
            away into the throat
            of the next tunnel.

IV
HELSINKI DRIFT

HELSINKI DRIFT

The accent's on the first syllable. The accent's
On the jewel-blue mid-June harbour. Masts,

Greased spars, gasoline streaks. A car ferry,
Far off, some sparkly white floating lozenge,

The ocean so magnificently
Stretched. Silent, vinyl. Here, slapping

Keels, it's rehearsing for a rather lax solstice,
Reluctant to glint under the common flapping

Of chesty, chocolate-faced gulls, green
Market awnings and boxed, flaked salt herring,

Belgian strawberries, cherries, juice-
Loosened butterflies (white chains of spray)

Twisting past the blind woman in a green dress
Torturing a violin. Her milk eyes

Clear when coins falling hit
Others in the hat at her feet. *Kitos*.

The accent shifts to midnight.
Midnight sunlight, midnight blindness.

SOPHIA

for Miglena Nicolchina

The mangy wisdom of wild dogs on every street,
skulking, pawing rabid piles of garbage
choking gutters, begging at the front doors of restaurants
like reeducated ideologues;
the battered wisdom of Ladas sputtering diesel-ink clouds;
the fickle wisdom of the dollar the pound the deutschmark
launching the price of turnips into orbit;
the ragged wisdom of dark Gypsy eyes;
the wizened wisdom of an old man's only arm
holding out a single ear of wizened corn,
quietly trying to sell the half-dozen kernels on it;
the rusted-out wisdom of a tram's Coke logo,
sparks flinting out from wheels that shriek
into the streets at sulphurous dusk;
the unpredictable wisdom of power failures, darkness at noon,
darkness at three, darkness at five, darkness
in crossed lines, voiceless telephone calls;
the Cyrillic wisdom of jazz saxophone
and democratic stars sparkling over Elinpelinstrasse;
the allegorical wisdom of Tom and Jerry on state TV;
the bacterial wisdom of yogurt curdling like truth into cliché;
the bitter wisdom of sediment in Turkish coffee;
the cellar-bar wisdom of cigarette smoke thick in the throat (air
like blue makeup
lurking in jeans the next morning);
the somersault wisdom of a three-year-old asking
if trees make the wind blow;
the fossilized wisdom of the Economic Recovery Laboratory,
the Committee for Mass Privatization;

the exiled wisdom of Kristeva living a Bulgarian afterlife
in Paris, her new look for "the mother"
in perpetual migration writing the totalitarian body;
the one-eyed wisdom of a steel guitarist (no amp)
covering "Tiny Bubbles," drinking 12% beer
in front of the National History Museum, Yeats's
Byzantium inside in ruins, no gold birds singing
their bodies electric anywhere in the dank, grim shadows;
the calculated wisdom of bribes—small bribes
to get into the country,
big bribes to get out; to look the other way
when a truckload of respirators and painkillers
roars off toward Istanbul in the dark;
the lip-synched wisdom of Orpheus,
Thracian karaoke commissar,
"this week at the Swingin' Hall,
the Black Sea's baddest nightclub";
the white wisdom of the moon
over the oldtown of Plovdiv, tall
Roman pillars throwing August shadows of empire
toward the third millennium;
the neon wisdom of a Lucky Strike sign, red beacon high
over the cold February street, students commanding police
to put guns down under bronzed WW II Russian soldiers;
the calculated wisdom of 100 questions for 100 days;
the crucified wisdom of Tartar-Greek-Madonna eyes;
the billboard wisdom of soles sliding
into black satin Versace pumps,
a black silk Versace blouse unbuttoned, nothing
under there but Swiss-psychoanalyzed breasts,
downy Reichean tension radiating along the sternum;
the black-market wisdom of caviar and vodka;

the peasant wisdom of donkeys pulling carts across country ruts
and goat-herd shepherds squatting in the shade
of chestnut canopies;
the air-conditioned wisdom of this immaculate black Mercedes
slicing through the crumbling streets,
your head resting guiltless on my chest
light as an Orthodox icon.

QUAI MIMOSA, SAINT-PIERRE

September moonlight, cool, a few stars start
dropping in, diamond
elegant through the famous mist, skip
three, four times
across the postcard harbour, glance
off masts toward red-blinking
beacons on l'Île aux Marins.

Six hundred shipwrecks?
Of course making it back was always miraculous.
After storms men would break
their precious, fired, net-needle-carved
clay pipes
across gunnels and drop them over the side, offerings
to *notre dame*: their names
wouldn't be washed up
onto the priest's brackish list
this time.

The bell-tower lamp
must have looked like the painted candle
in *la crèche*
from the very last pew of the church
la veille de Noël.
Handing the glass
eye to eye, everything enlarged
slowed down except
hearts, detonating
shouts from hooded women kneeling
who made themselves believe

what they saw
wasn't some ghost ship
tethered to the moon.

WAITING FOR THE ANAHITRA

It can say "fossil" on my left
wrist, and that's apparently all the time
I'll have to recall her two basic sleeping positions,
breathing patterns, nails
painted the colour of orchids in a pine grotto,
unadjustable contrast, hotel-room
TV, Agassi smashing a backhand overhead
cross-court volley for a winner, deuce…
all the time left before palpitations
provide a new measure
and the poem writes me
out of itself, out of the hunger
for hurricane news and pizza chèvrette,
with "conditions variable," overdrawn
to the limit, faxing across borders, one big
ocean, respecting the five-second delay
as my voice leaves
the cable, then the planet, bounces
into orbit, down to Paris back up
and across and down, all this
acrostic circuitry just to reach
Halifax, here's to circumlocution
in a brown leather jacket (just as
sandals also should always be brown),
when just to kill an hour walking
to the lighthouse is too far, or the cemetery
where they bury their dead
aboveground, the whitewashed headstones
from here could be paint specks
in your hair, on a ladder,

hunched under soffit and fascia, finishing
trim, bigger blotches of white
on the back of your neck, smaller
ones (you're in cutoffs) above the knee, the left,
because you're a southpaw,
and so is your syntax, rungs
of sexual remembrance, undressing for the bath,
alternating legs, soaped,
held straight up out of the water
shaving the hair down to
nubs of candlelight, humming
nothing because by that time the new moon
had proven to be too much
for the beginning of the month
and all the words we'd once found useful
had taken early retirement.

Miquelon

SHRINE OF NOTRE DAME, MODELLED ON LOURDES, L'ÎLE AUX MARINS, SAINT-PIERRE

The drowned
know better.
This water
does not
heal.

Should I just stand here until dark and attract
lightning? "Tell me about it."

I could turn around and leave
the waves to their little games,

cross the hot asphalt of place Général de Gaulle
and grab some chicken at *l'express snack*.

The air's so thick women are
crossing themselves as they descend

the ramp off the ferry from Miquelon.
Cigar smoke floats and hovers from

somewhere. From somewhere perfume
ferries me through memory, arc
of a slender bicep transporting
on a silver tray
espresso and croissants and jam and sugar and

wind from Montpellier not so dry
as to conspire against

the scent of June trapped
where her tan line and white cotton

scoop neckline defined
desire and its uncrossable border—

how I wanted
to walk off the end

of *that* pier and fall
"into her life"

if only for the moment
it took to learn

the words in her language for
"is a storm coming?"

GIOTTO IN COLORADO: FUTURE WORK, SHALE SERIES

He's gotten here, stunned and breathless, because
there's divine interest owing
from all the grace
he captured in gestures of light, paint, dreams, sweat
plastered on the rich walls of Firenze—
and he is it.
Substantiated, he's lost the balance
that could have saved him from this. Christ,
I'm Christ, he thinks, looking for holes
in his hands. This is the punishment
for doubt? The reward for lust?

(Rust light pours itself into him
through his intrigued arms that knew
this had to happen, the way they'd known
caresses, inviting more,
fuelled by disaster.)

In the copper hogbacks, cragged against a leftover voyageur
chine colle paper-blue sky, he sees layered
trecento shale-engraved depictions of Egypt and the Exodus:
three angels in chaps and Stetsons hover in broad, whooshy
strokes above wind-battered, ripple-robed Moses
in the cartoon stagecoach of a cloud,
Storm Mountain splits,
spits out a coyote pharaoh in black cape segmented
like a coral snake against a pyramid
in chiaroscuro cross-hatching, but he can't
find his tower, his green marble

dream shadowing the Duomo. There is only the shadow
of a hawk, small black gash
moving across the limit of the world
high over Colorado, and Giotto wonders
what godforsaken regiment has been assigned this
dust-ridden duty. And, indeed, if God
has placed him here as some merciful reinstatement,
it is a cruel accommodation. What work
will fall as evidence of his cowboy dispensation
will be work of simple agony, left
as if it were standing in the central courtyard
of the Pitti, a titanic tribute to anachronism
in glazed shale (guaranteeing decrepitude), tribute
to pain, a god of pain:
enormous, fractured head, blotted
eyes, taut cheeks, taut lips,
the garish angle of the neck continually
forced under its unsupportable weight,
emaciated chest, swollen abdomen,
wasted, veined muscles in the arms and thighs,
knobbed joints, lumps suppurating
through Calvin Klein cotton
at the groin—love in deformity, awakened.

And when it's complete, he'll have paid
the debt, and the heavens *will* actually open
and he'll be raptured up
in some archangel's ATV
to the strains of a honky-tonk jukebox choir's
Deus qui sedes super thronum
past the snowy indigo peaks
toward a hand that's reaching down
as if picking up a dropped toy.

NIGHT TRAIL, HOME: ANTI-TITLE HAIKU

The trail curved perfect
as a promise
to the dark

Moonlight
fell partial to
trail glaze, pine
shadows black on tracked snow

The silence (only virtual)
couldn't prevent
friction's stammer

I slept to hear
a mirage of stars
soak up midnight
dreamed a title
for the ideal
moving through the actual

Douglas Burnet Smith is the author of ten previous volumes of poetry, including *The Killed* and *Chainletter*. He received a Governor General's Award poetry nomination for *Voices from a Farther Room* and has won *The Malahat Review*'s Long Poem Prize, as well as other awards. Currently he divides his time between Paris, France, and Antigonish, Nova Scotia, where he teaches at St. Francis Xavier University.

MORE NEW POETRY FROM BEACH HOLME

Iron Mountain
by Mark Frutkin
POETRY $12.95 CDN $8.95 US ISBN: 0-88878-424-4

Divided into two sections, one inspired by ancient Chinese art, the other limning the ambiguities and incongruities of the contemporary human condition, Frutkin's new volume of poetry, *Iron Mountain,* often presents human beings wandering in the wilderness between two abysses while still appreciating the smell of pines, the softness of the rain, the brilliance of the stars, the hum of the computer, and the jostle of the crowd on the bus.

Prime
by Miranda Pearson
POETRY $12.95 CDN $8.95 US ISBN: 0-88878-418-X

In *Prime*, the narratives of female identity, the white wedding, and the enshrined position of the mother are interrogated, using the lyric as a form of cultural critique in an examination and mockery of romantic love and heterosexual relationships. At the same time, the poems constitute an irreverent, lush romp, a celebration of friendship and absurdity.

Purity of Absence
by Dave Margoshes
POETRY $12.95 CDN $8.95 US ISBN: 0-88878-419-8

In *Purity of Absence*, Dave Margoshes explores love in its waxing and waning, the extravagance of its fullness, the agony of its departure. Like an explorer charting new territory, he casts his eye on the rhythms and syntax of love, observing its aspects both quotidian and rare. The poems in this new collection, Margoshes's first in a decade, chart the EKG patterns of love, not just the mature love between a man and a woman but love for a parent, friends, knowledge, place and, ultimately, life itself.

BEACH HOLME PUBLISHING ♦ WWW.BEACHHOLME.BC.CA